SCHOLASTIC
News
Nonfiction Readers

Who Works at the Zoo?

By Alyse Sweeney

Children's Press®
A Division of Scholastic Inc.
New York Toronto London Auckland Sydney
Mexico City New Delhi Hong Kong
Danbury, Connecticut

These content vocabulary word builders are for grades 1–2.

Reading Consultant: Cecilia Minden-Cupp, PhD, Former Director of the Language and Literacy Program, Harvard Graduate School of Education, Cambridge, Massachusetts

Photographs © 2007: Alamy Images/MedioImages: 21 top; AP/Wide World Photos: 4 bottom left, 10 (Bob Hallinen/Anchorage Daily News), 4 bottom right, 8 (Cathal McNaughton/PA); Bruce Coleman Inc./Stephen Kline: 9; Corbis Images: 4 top, 19 (B. Bird/zefa), 20 top (Tom Brakefield), 23 top right (Stephen Frink), back cover, 5 bottom left, 15 (Karen Kasmauski), 5 bottom right, 7 (Stephanie Maze), 23 top left (Joe McDonald), 11 (Richard T. Nowitz), 21 bottom (Galen Rowell), 2, 5 top right, 12, 23 bottom left (Royalty-Free), 23 bottom right (Kevin Schafer), 20 bottom (Michael S. Yamashita); Minden Pictures/Katherine Feng/Globio: 13; Zoological Society of San Diego: cover, 1, 5 top left, 17.

Book Design: Simonsays Design!
Book Production: The Design Lab

Library of Congress Cataloging-in-Publication Data

Sweeney, Alyse.
    Who works at the zoo? / Alyse Sweeney.
        p. cm. — (Scholastic news nonfiction readers)
    Includes bibliographical references and index.
    ISBN-10: 0-531-16842-5
    ISBN-13: 978-0-531-16842-4
    1. Zoo keepers—Juvenile literature. I. Title. II. Series.
    QL50.5.S94 2007
    590.73—dc22   2006015652

1 2 3 4 5 6 7 8 9 10 R 16 15 14 13 12 11 10 09 08 07

CONTENTS

WORD HUNT

Look for these words as you read. They will be in **bold**.

beluga whale
(beh-**loo**-guh **wayle**)

meals
(meels)

report
(ri-**port**)

4

caretaker
(**kair**-tay-kur)

habitat
(**hab**-uh-tat)

veterinarian
(vet-er-e-**nare**-ee-un)

zookeeper
(**zu**-keep-uhr)

Teamwork at the Zoo

It takes many people working together to make a zoo run smoothly.

First, let's meet a **zookeeper**.

Splish, splash! The zookeeper gives this elephant a bath.

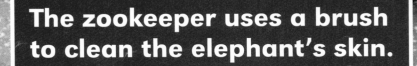

The zookeeper uses a brush to clean the elephant's skin.

Zookeepers feed the animals, too.

Zookeepers also watch the animals each day and write a **report**. In a report, the zookeeper writes how the animals act and what they eat.

report

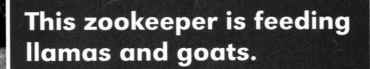
This zookeeper is feeding llamas and goats.

Workers prepare food for the animals in a big kitchen. They make hundreds of **meals** each day.

Fruits, vegetables, chicken, fish, peanut butter, and hay are all found in the kitchen.

meals

Look at all the different foods in the zoo kitchen!

Animals aren't that different from us. They like playing, too!

Zookeepers try to get the animals to play in their zoo **habitat**, or home.

habitat

This panda is having a fun time swinging through the air!

Zoo animals get regular checkups and teeth cleanings, just like people do. When they are sick, they need special care.

Whose job is it to make sure zoo animals are healthy? A **veterinarian**!

This veterinarian is about to listen to the panda's heartbeat.

What happens at the zoo's hospital? A **caretaker** raises baby animals.

This gorilla's mother was not able to care for her. A caretaker acts like the gorilla's mother until she is ready to join the other gorillas.

A caretaker feeds this baby gorilla a bottle of milk.

Everyone at the zoo works together to make sure the animals stay healthy.

They care for this **beluga whale**, which is endangered.

What a job!

FEEDING TIME AT THE ZOO

An **anteater** at the zoo may eat ants, termites, and fruit. It digs for insects in dirt mounds and logs.

A **crocodile** at the zoo may eat rats, mice, and chicken parts.

A **giraffe** at the zoo may eat leaves, hay, and carrots.

A **mountain goat** at the zoo may eat different grasses and hay.

YOUR NEW WORDS

beluga whale (beh-**loo**-guh **wayle**) a large, white whale

caretaker (**kair**-tay-kur) a person who cares for baby animals at a zoo

habitat (**hab**-uh-tat) where a plant or animal usually lives

meals (meels) foods that are eaten at a certain time

report (ri-**port**) a description or a statement

veterinarian (vet-er-e-**nare**-ee-un) an animal doctor

zookeeper (**zu**-keep-uhr) a person who cares for animals at a zoo

OTHER ANIMALS AT THE ZOO

boa constrictor

dolphin

lion

toucan

INDEX

FIND OUT MORE
Book:
Fowler, Allan. *Animals in the Zoo.* New York: Children's Press, 2000.

Website:
San Diego Zoo Kid Territory
http://www.sandiegozoo.org/kids/

MEET THE AUTHOR:
Alyse Sweeney is a freelance writer who has published more than twenty books and poems for children. Prior to becoming a freelance writer, she was a teacher, reading specialist, and Scholastic editor. Alyse lives in Las Vegas, Nevada, with her husband and two children.